An American School Day

Dona Herweck Rice

Going to School

walking

biking

taking
a bus

using a crosswalk

being dropped off

driving

Morning Routines

eat breakfast

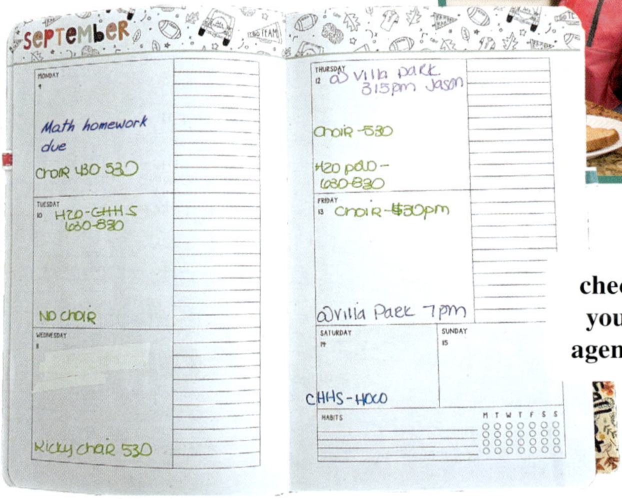

check your agenda

greet friends

homeroom

announcements

Pledge of Allegiance

language arts

math

physical education (PE)

science

social
studies

elective

notebook

binder

folders

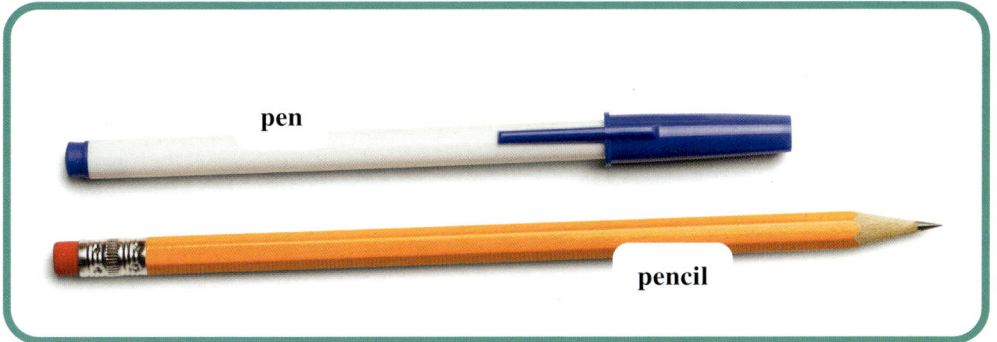
pen

pencil

student
ID

012 345 678 9

backpack

Reading and Writing

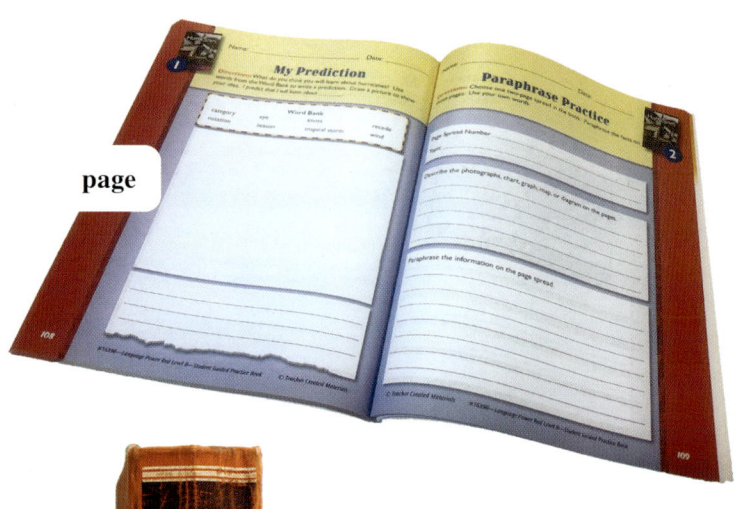

page

nonfiction

book

fiction

essay

Shall I compare thee to a summer's day? Thou art more lovely & more temperate: Rough winds do shake the darling buds of May And Summer's lease hath all too short a date: Some time too hot the eye of heaven shines, And often is his gold complexion dimm'd: And every fair from fair sometimes declines,

poetry

Changing Classes

lockers

time

water
fountatins

restrooms

hallway

walk, don't run

Learning

study

research

group

project

partners

class

Lunch

cafeteria

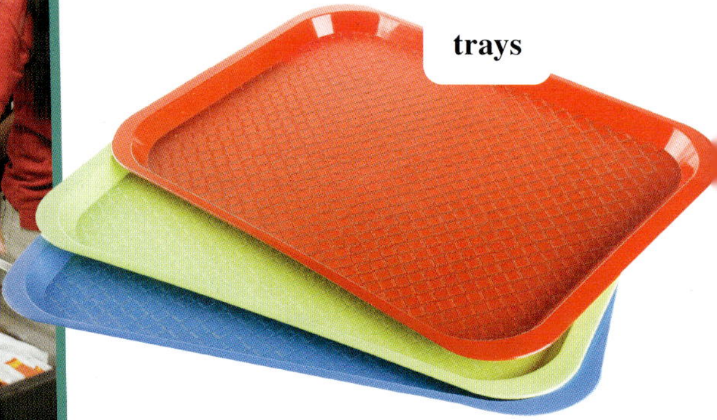

trays

Port Huron North[e]

eating

drinking

being with friends

cleaning up

17

Important People to Know

students

teacher

counselor

principal

security officer

custodian

office

classroom

auditorium

library

gym

campus

Equipment

desks and chairs

computers

whiteboard

bulletin board

sports equipment

rally

drill

performance

assembly

game

dance

store things

pack your bag

say goodbye

get
a
ride

Angeles High School

parking
lot

go
home

club

job

sports

homework

lessons

tutoring

Helping at Home

caring for pets

caring for siblings

helping family

doing
chores

running
errands

cooking

Consultant

Janessa Lang, M.A.Ed.
Elementary Teacher, Los Angeles

Publishing Credits

Rachelle Cracchiolo, M.S.Ed., *Publisher*
Emily R. Smith, M.A.Ed., *SVP of Content Development*
Véronique Bos, *VP of Creative*
Robin Erickson, *Senior Art Director*

Photo Credits: p.5, Alamy; p.11, Dona Rice; p.16, Alamy; p.23, Cassie Labriola-Sitzman;
p.24–26,Getty Images; all other images from iStock, Shutterstock, or in the public domain.

Library of Congress Control Number available upon request

5482 Argosy Avenue
Huntington Beach, CA 92649
www.tcmpub.com
ISBN 979-8-3309-0485-3
© 2025 Teacher Created Materials, Inc.
Printed by: 51497
Printed in: China